The Countries

Argentina

Kate A. Conley

ABDO Publishing Company

visit us at
www.abdopub.com

Published by ABDO Publishing Company, 4940 Viking Drive, Edina, Minnesota 55435.
Copyright © 2004 by Abdo Consulting Group, Inc. International copyrights reserved in
all countries. No part of this book may be reproduced in any form without written
permission from the publisher.

Printed in the United States.

Photo Credits: Corbis pp. 5, 6, 8, 9, 10, 11, 13, 16, 18, 19, 21, 22, 23, 24, 26, 27, 29, 30,
     31, 32-33, 35, 36, 37

Editors: Stephanie Hedlund, Kristianne E. Vieregger
Art Direction & Maps: Neil Klinepier

Library of Congress Cataloging-in-Publication Data

Conley, Kate A., 1977-
    Argentina / Kate A. Conley.
       p. cm. -- (The countries)
    Includes index.
    Summary: An introduction to the history, geography, plants and animals, people,
economy, cities, transportation, government, holidays and festivals, and culture of
Argentina.
    ISBN 1-59197-290-6
     1. Argentina--Juvenile literature. [1. Argentina.] I. Title. II. Series.

F2808.2.C66 2003
982--dc21
                                                        2003040340

Contents

¡Hola!

Hello from Argentina! When Spaniards first arrived on this land, they thought it was rich in silver. So, they named it Argentina, which means "land of silver." Explorers did not find as much silver as they had hoped. However, they did find a land rich in many other ways.

Argentina is a country of beauty and **culture**. Its people have created dances, writings, and foods unlike anywhere else on Earth. Its festivals and holidays also reflect the **unique** nature of this society.

Throughout its history, Argentina has survived many difficult events. A war of independence, waves of **immigration**, and military governments have shaped the nation. Through it all, Argentines have maintained a positive spirit. Today, they look forward to a bright future.

Hola *from Argentina!*

Fast Facts

BUENOS AIRES

OFFICIAL NAME: Argentine Republic
(República Argentina)
CAPITAL: Buenos Aires

LAND
- Area: 1,068,302 square miles (2,766,890 sq km)
- Mountain Range: Andes Mountains
- Highest Point: Cerro Aconcagua 22,835 feet (6,960 m)
- Major Rivers: Paraná, Uruguay, and Iguazú Rivers

PEOPLE
- Population: 37,812,817 (July 2002 est.)
- Major Cities: Buenos Aires, Córdoba
- Languages: Spanish (official), English, Italian, German, and French
- Religions: Roman Catholicism, Protestantism, and Judaism

GOVERNMENT
- Form: Republic
- Head of State: President
- Legislature: National Congress
- Nationhood: July 9, 1816

ECONOMY
- Agricultural Products: Sunflower seeds, lemons, soybeans, grapes, corn, tobacco, peanuts, tea, wheat; livestock
- Mining Products: Natural gas, coal, uranium, lead, zinc, silver, copper, manganese, tungsten
- Manufactured Products: Food products, textiles, steel
- Money: Argentine peso (1 peso = 100 centavos)

Argentina's flag

Paper version of the Argentine peso

Timeline

1500s	Europeans start exploring Argentina
1535	Spain sends an expedition to settle in Argentina
1553	Settlers establish Argentina's first permanent Spanish settlement
1600s	Settlers establish large ranches managed by gauchos
1816	Argentina declares its independence from Spain
1860-1940	More than 3.5 million Europeans immigrate to Argentina
1943	Juan Perón overthrows Argentina's government
1946	Perón elected president
1955	Perón removed from office
1976	Military overthrows government; the Dirty War begins
1983	Military steps down; Raúl Alfosín works to improve economy
1990s	Argentina's debt grows; the economy weakens
2001	Raised taxes and cut programs lead to protests

Argentina's History

The first people to live in Argentina were Indians. Then in the 1500s, Europeans began exploring Argentina. One explorer, Sebastian Cabot, reported that the land was rich in silver.

In 1535, Spain sent an **expedition** to Argentina. This expedition, led by Pedro de Mendoza, worked to settle the land. However, Indian attacks and a lack of food discouraged these settlers.

Sebastian Cabot

People from nearby Spanish colonies soon arrived in Argentina. In fact, settlers from Peru established Argentina's first permanent Spanish settlement in 1553. It was called Santiago del Estero (san-tee-AH-goh del uh-STEHR-oh).

In the 1600s, settlers were granted large plots of land in the Pampas. There, they established ranches called *estancias*. The ranchers hired gauchos (GOW-choz). Gauchos managed the cattle and horses that ran wild on the land. Over time, gauchos came to represent the spirit of Argentina.

A gaucho watches over a herd of cattle.

Spain ruled Argentina for nearly 300 years. Then on July 9, 1816, Argentines declared their independence. This led to several years of fighting. Finally, Spain was defeated.

Argentines tried to form a national government. However, several local leaders fought for control. Then, Juan Manuel de Rosas began ruling as a **dictator**. He led the nation from 1835 to 1852.

Shortly after Rosas's rule, many **immigrants** arrived in Argentina. In fact, more than 3.5 million Europeans moved to Argentina between 1860 and 1940. Most of the immigrants were Italian or Spanish.

Immigrants slept in these beds when they first arrived in Argentina around 1900.

In 1943, a military leader named Juan Perón (WHAN pay-ROHN) overthrew Argentina's government. Three years later, Argentines elected Perón president. He became famous for his efforts to help the working class. Perón's wife, Eva, was also well known. She worked to empower Argentine women.

Perón ruled Argentina until 1955, when the military removed him from office. The next 20 years were difficult for Argentines. The **economy** weakened, few people had jobs, and the government changed often.

Juan and Eva Perón

In 1976, the military overtook Argentina's government again. It closed the congress, **censored** the people, and banned unions. The new government killed or tortured more than 10,000 scholars, artists, and political leaders. This time period is known as the Dirty War.

The military stepped down in 1983. Raúl Alfonsín (rah-OOL ahl-fohn-SEEN) became the next president. He worked to correct the military's abuses. He also tried to improve the **economy**. The next president, Carlos Saúl Menem (KAHR-lohs SAWL MEH-nehm), continued this work.

Despite these efforts, a huge **debt** loomed over Argentina. As a result, the government raised taxes and cut programs. This led to massive strikes. In 2001, Argentina's president, Fernando de la Rua (fehr-NAHN-doh day lah ROO-ah), stepped down.

Today, Argentines face an uncertain future. Their leaders must reduce the debt and create a healthy, stable economy. In the meantime, the people must draw upon their own resources to strengthen their beloved nation.

Fernando de la Rua stops to visit with children while on the campaign trail.

Rugged Landscape

Argentina is located in South America. It is South America's second-largest country. Only Brazil is larger. Argentina's vast area has many different types of land.

Argentina's land differs from north to south. Northern Argentina is made up of lowlands. Central Argentina contains grassy plains called the Pampas. Southern Argentina, called Patagonia, contains **steppes** leading to the Atlantic Ocean.

Mountains are another major feature in Argentina. The Andes Mountains are located along Argentina's western border. They stretch the entire length of the country.

Many rivers flow through Argentina, too. In central Argentina, the Paraná (pah-rah-NAH) and Uruguay

North

West — East

South

North
America

Asia

Europe

Africa

South
America

**DETAIL
AREA**

Australia

Antarctica

(oo-roo-GWI) Rivers meet. There, they form the Río de la Plata (REE-oh day la PLAH-tah). It is a major **estuary** of the Atlantic Ocean.

The Iguazú (ee-gwah-SOO) River is also important. It flows over a large **escarpment** near the border of Argentina, Brazil, and Paraguay. This forms Iguazú Falls. They are some of the world's most spectacular waterfalls.

In general, Argentina's climate is mild. However, the land in the southeast is very dry. In the southwest, the land is very cold. Southern Argentina receives little rain. But, rain is more plentiful in some parts of the north.

Iguazú Falls

Rainfall

AVERAGE YEARLY RAINFALL

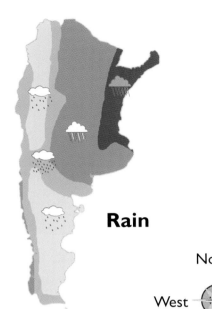

Rain

Inches		*Centimeters*
Under 10		*Under 25*
10 - 20		*25 - 51*
20 - 40		*51 - 102*
Over 40		*Over 102*

North

West — — East

South

Temperature

AVERAGE TEMPERATURE

Winter

Fahrenheit		*Celsius*
Over 80°		*Over 27°*
65° - 80°		*18° - 27°*
50° - 65°		*10° - 18°*
32° - 50°		*0° - 10°*
Below 32°		*Below 0°*

Summer

Plants & Animals

Argentina has a large variety of plants and animals. In the north, much of the land is dry. Shrubs and grasses grow in this area. Animals such as llamas, alpacas, and vicuñas (vih-KOON-yuhs) live there, too.

The land between the Paraná and Uruguay Rivers receives plenty of rain. Forests grow in this area. This provides **habitats** for many animals. They include jaguars, monkeys, deer, and many species of birds.

The Pampas of central Argentina are grasslands. The grasses often grow knee high. Animals that live there include the guanaco (gwuh-NAH-koh) and the rhea. The guanaco is a

A guanaco

large mammal related to the camel. The rhea is a large bird that cannot fly. It is similar to an ostrich.

In Patagonia, the land is filled with shrubs and grasses. Some parts of Patagonia also contain forests of beech trees. Guanacos, rheas, eagles, herons, hares, and mountain cats live in this region.

A rhea

Argentines

The first people to live in Argentina were Indians. After Spanish explorers arrived, many Indians died. Today, about 100,000 Indians live in Argentina. The largest groups are the Quechua (KEH-chuh-wuh) and the Mapuche.

Most of the other people living in Argentina have European roots. That's because millions of Europeans **immigrated** to Argentina. Most immigrants were Italian or Spanish. Other immigrants included German, French, and English people.

Argentines speak Spanish. It is the country's official language. However, people speak other languages, too. These include English, Italian, German, and French.

Argentine festivals often celebrate the country's culture. These people are enjoying a gaucho festival with dancing and costumes.

Many churches can be found in Buenos Aires and in other cities throughout Argentina.

Most Argentines are Roman Catholic. It is the country's official religion. The country's many **immigrants** brought the Protestant and Jewish faiths to Argentina, too.

Education in Argentina is free. Children ages six through 14 must attend primary school. Students may then choose to continue their education. About half of all students attend secondary school.

Argentines live in many kinds of homes. In Argentina's large cities, people often live in apartment buildings. In the **suburbs**, people live in houses.

At home, Argentines cook many different kinds of food. The most common food is beef. A popular way to prepare beef is by grilling it. This meat is also eaten in stews, casseroles, and sandwiches.

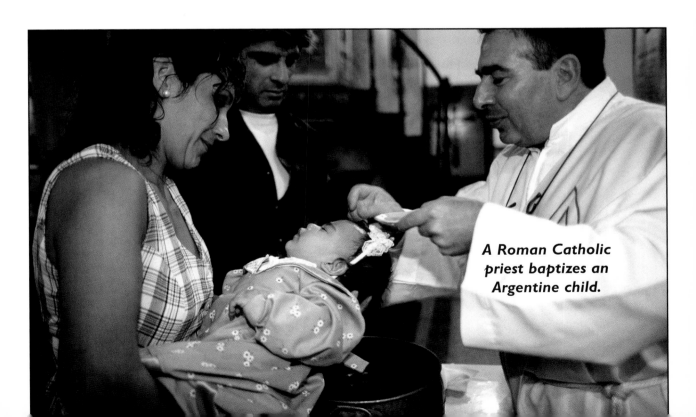

A Roman Catholic priest baptizes an Argentine child.

Argentines often drink maté (MAH-tay). To prepare it, dried maté leaves are placed in a special gourd. Hot water is poured over them. Then, a silver straw is placed in the gourd. The straw has a filter on it. This stops the leaves from entering the straw.

Maté can taste bitter at first, but after a few tries, most people are sure to enjoy the experience.

Chimichurri

Chimichurri is a sauce that is used on grilled meats in Argentina.

- 1 cup olive oil
- 1/3 cup chopped onions
- 1 bunch chopped parsley
- 1 teaspoon cayenne pepper

- 1/2 cup vinegar
- 1 clove garlic, chopped
- 1 teaspoon oregano
- Salt and pepper to taste

Mix the oil and vinegar in a bowl. Stir in remaining ingredients. Serve with your favorite grilled meat.

AN IMPORTANT NOTE TO THE CHEF: Always have an adult help with the preparation and cooking of food. Never use kitchen utensils or appliances without adult permission and supervision.

English	Spanish
Hello	Hola (OH-lah)
Please	Por Favor (POHR fah-VOHR)
Girl	Chica (CHEE-kah)
Boy	Chico (CHEE-koh)
Friend	Amigo/Amiga (ah-MEE-goh/ah-MEE-gah)

LANGUAGE

Hard at Work

Argentines work in many different jobs. Some work as farmers, providing food for their country. Others manufacture goods that people use every day.

Farming is especially important to Argentina's **economy**. Argentina exports more food than any other country in **Latin America**. Wheat, corn, sorghum, and soybeans are the main crops.

Herding cattle

Some farmers also raise animals. Cattle ranches are common in the Pampas. Meat from cattle is one of Argentina's most valuable exports. Farmers also raise sheep and pigs.

The products from Argentina's farms are manufactured into goods. For example, workers mill wheat into flour. And they process cattle into hides, leather, and canned meat.

Buyers shop for fresh vegetables in an Argentine market.

Beginning in the 1940s, Argentina's government tried to expand the nation's industries. Today, Argentine factories produce many different goods. Some of the newer products manufactured include **petroleum** products, cement, steel, and iron.

Buenos Aires & Beyond

Buenos Aires (bway-nohs-EYE-rays) is Argentina's capital and largest city. It is located along the shores of the Río de la Plata. More than 8 million people live in Buenos Aires and its **suburbs**. These people have created a **diverse** and prosperous city.

Buenos Aires is a mix of European and **Latin-American** influences. For example, some areas look as if they belong in Paris, France. Other areas have **unique** Latin-American features, such as tango salons.

The Plaza de Mayo is a **landmark** in Buenos Aires. The plaza has attractive fountains and palm trees. Nearby are several historic buildings. One of them, the Casa Rosada, is the presidential palace.

Córdoba (KOHR-doh-bah) is Argentina's second-largest city. More than 1 million people live there. In the 1600s, Córdoba was a political, **economic**, and **cultural** center. Today, Córdoba is still a bustling city.

Buenos Aires

From Place to Place

Argentines have many ways to travel. In Buenos Aires, for example, people can ride the Subte (SOOB-tay). It is South America's oldest subway system. Despite its age, the Subte is still a quick way to get around the city.

Since Argentina is so large, some people take an airplane when traveling long distances. All major cities have airports. Aerolíneas Argentinas is the country's most important airline. It offers local and international flights.

Buses are another way people travel in Argentina. Most towns have a central bus station. From there, buses travel to nearly every part of the country.

Most flights in and out of the country go through Ezeiza International Airport.

Ships are also important forms of transportation. Oceangoing ships transport Argentina's goods to other countries. Smaller ships carry passengers and goods to Argentina's coastal cities.

Taking the bus is a convenient way to travel through Argentina.

Governing the Republic

Argentina's government is a **republic**. Its federal capital is the city of Buenos Aires. The republic is also made up of 23 **provinces**. Each province has a local government led by a governor, lawmakers, and judges.

Nationally, a president governs Argentina. The president is the leader of the military. The president also appoints people to the Cabinet of Ministers. It oversees the day-to-day running of the country.

Argentina's lawmakers are part of the National Congress. It is divided into two bodies, the Senate and the Chamber of Deputies. Members of the National Congress create and pass Argentina's laws.

The highest court in Argentina is the Supreme Court. It is made up of nine judges. The president appoints the judges to this court, and the Senate approves them.

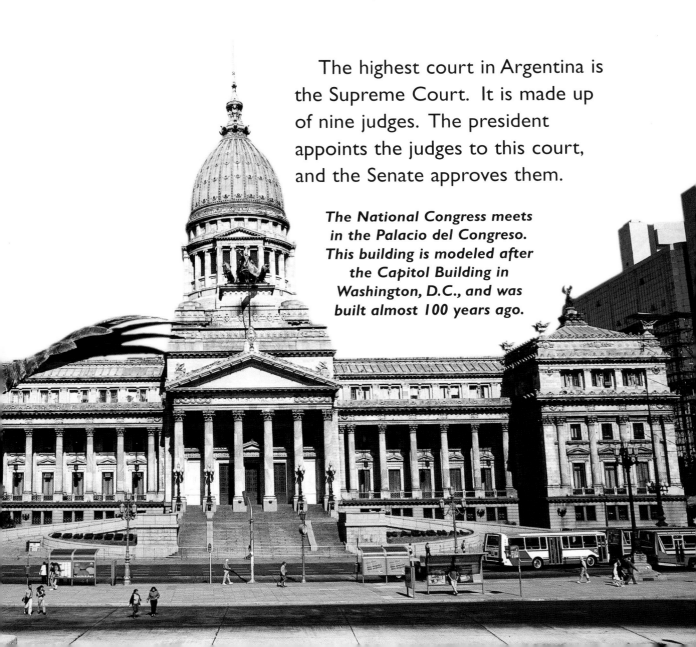

The National Congress meets in the Palacio del Congreso. This building is modeled after the Capitol Building in Washington, D.C., and was built almost 100 years ago.

Time to Celebrate!

Argentines celebrate many holidays. Some holidays, such as Christmas, are religious. Others are national holidays, such as Independence Day.

Many Argentines spend Christmas with their families. Often, they attend a church service together. Common Christmas treats are called *niños envueltos* (NEE-nyohs en-VWAYL-tohs). They are small pieces of beef filled with eggs, onions, spices, and mincemeat.

Another popular holiday is Carnaval. It is celebrated a week before **Lent**. During Carnaval, people attend large parades. Children have water balloon fights. Folk music and dancing are also common.

On July 9, Argentines celebrate Independence Day. It is the date that General José de San Martín declared Argentina independent from Spain. Celebrations are especially lively in Tucumán, where San Martín made his declaration.

Musicians at a gaucho festival

Argentine Culture

Argentines have created a **unique culture**. Argentina is most famous for the tango. It is a ballroom dance. The tango alternates between long, gliding steps and short, quick steps.

Jorge Luis Borges

Argentina is also famous for its many talented writers. One of Argentina's best-known writers is Jorge Luis Borges (HOHR-hay loo-EES BOHR-hays). He wrote poetry, short stories, and novels. Often, his writing dealt with everyday life in Argentina.

Reading is important to many Argentines. Every April, Buenos Aires hosts South America's largest book fair. Besides books, Argentina also produces many magazines and newspapers. Two newspapers, *La Prensa* and *La Nación*, are world famous.

Throughout Argentina, people enjoy sports. By far, soccer is the most popular sport. Bicycling is also growing in popularity. In the summer, people take bike trips around the country. It is a great way for Argentines to get out and enjoy their beautiful homeland!

The tango can be a difficult dance to master. Tango salons can be found in most cities within Argentina.

Glossary

censor - to suppress or remove material that is considered offensive.

culture - the customs, arts, and tools of a nation or people at a certain time.

debt - something owed to someone, usually money.

dictator - a ruler with complete control who usually governs in a cruel or unfair way.

diverse - composed of several distinct pieces or qualities.

economy - the way a nation uses its money, goods, and natural resources.

escarpment - a steep slope or cliff.

estuary - the body of water where a river's current meets an ocean's tide.

expedition - a journey for a special purpose, such as exploration or scientific study.

habitat - a place where a living thing is naturally found.

immigration - entry into another country to live. A person who immigrates is called an immigrant.

landmark - an important structure of historical or physical interest.

Latin America - the region including Mexico, Central America, South America, and the West Indies.

Lent - the 40 weekdays before Easter.

petroleum - a thick, yellowish black oil. It is used to make gasoline.
province - a geographical or governmental division of a country.
republic - a form of government in which authority rests with voting citizens and is carried out by elected officials, such as those in a parliament.
steppe - an area of land that is usually level and treeless.
suburb - a town or village just outside a city.
unique - being the only one of its kind.

Web Sites

To learn more about Argentina, visit ABDO Publishing Company on the World Wide Web at **www.abdopub.com**. Web sites about Argentina are featured on our Book Links page. These links are routinely monitored and updated to provide the most current information available.

Index